Peace in th

MW01601757

Being Faithful in the Chaos of Calling, Kids, and Everyday Life

By William E. Jackson

"These things I have spoken unto you, that in me ye might have peace.
In the world ye shall have tribulation: but be of good cheer;
I have overcome the world."
— **John 16:33 (KJV)**

Toombs County, Georgia
2025

Peace in the Pressure

Credits and Acknowledgments

Author:
Written by William E. Jackson

Cover Design:
Cover artwork created using Canva Pro, and DALL·E customized and formatted by the author.

Interior Layout & Design:
Formatted using Microsoft Word for self-publishing through Amazon KDP.

Scripture References:
All Scripture quotations are taken from the King James Version (KJV) of the Bible, which is in the public domain.

Fonts & Elements:
Fonts and design elements used within this book are licensed through Canva Pro and Microsoft Office or are in the public domain.

Tools Used:
This devotional was written and designed using Microsoft Word and Canva Pro. Final publishing was completed through Kindle Direct Publishing (KDP).

Special Thanks:

For my Savior, who brings Peace in the Pressure, and Calm in the Chaos, who walks through life's darkest moments and brings us out on the other side.

My Family, and My Friends who have supported me, helped me, and who walked through these deep moments with me. God Sees.

Introduction

Peace in the Pressure isn't just a title, it's a testimony.

If you're anything like me, life hasn't slowed down just because you believe in Jesus. The calling He placed on your life didn't come with a pause button. The bills still show up. The kids still need your attention. The job still demands your time. And somehow, in the middle of all of it, you're expected to be faithful.

This devotional was born out of pressure—real pressure. The kind that keeps you up at night wondering how to carry everything without falling apart. As a pastor, husband, father of four, and nonprofit director, I've been in that place where faith feels like the only thread holding me together.

That's why I wrote this. Not to offer cute clichés or empty encouragement, but to help you find peace in your own pressure. To remind you that God doesn't ask for perfection—He asks for surrender. And in the surrender, we find strength.

Over the next 21 days, we'll walk through stories, Scriptures, and moments from my own life and calling. Some of them were hard. Some were humbling. But through them all, God has been faithful—and I've learned how to be faithful in return.

So wherever you are in your journey—whether you're carrying a heavy load or just trying to survive the chaos—know this: you're not alone, and there is peace available, even here.

Let's take this journey together, and let's be faithful in the chaos of calling, kids, and everyday life.

~William Jackson

Table of Contents:

not seen."
— Hebrews 11:1 (KJV)

Day 7: Rest in His Peace

Scripture:
"Peace I leave with you, my peace I give unto you: not as the world giveth, give I unto you. Let not your heart be troubled, neither let it be afraid."
— John 14:27 (KJV)

Day 8: When You Feel Behind

Scripture:
"The steps of a good man are ordered by the Lord: and he delighteth in his way."
— Psalm 37:23 (KJV)

Day 9: Success Redefined

Scripture:
"But he that is greatest among you shall be your servant."
— Matthew 23:11 (KJV)

Day 10: Beauty in the Brokenness

Scripture:
"But he said to me, *My grace is sufficient for thee: for my strength is made perfect in weakness.* Most gladly therefore will I rather glory in my infirmities, that the power of Christ may rest upon me."
— 2 Corinthians 12:9 (KJV)

Day 11: *Called, but Not Always Comfortable*

Scripture:
"But the Lord said unto me, Say not, I am a child: for thou shalt go to all that I shall send thee, and whatsoever I command thee thou shalt speak. Be not afraid of their faces: for I am with thee to deliver thee, saith the Lord."
— Jeremiah 1:7–8 (KJV)

Day 12: *Faith in the Fog*

Scripture:
(For we walk by faith, not by sight:)
— 2 Corinthians 5:7 (KJV)

Day 13: *When the Applause Fades*

"And whatsoever ye do, do it heartily, as to the Lord, and not unto men;"
— Colossians 3:23 (KJV)

Day 14: Strong Enough to Stay

☐ Scripture:

Jeremiah 17:7-8 (KJV)

"Blessed is the man that trusteth in the Lord, and whose hope the Lord is. For he shall be as a tree planted by the waters, and that spreadeth out her roots by the river, and shall not see when heat cometh, but her leaf shall be green; and shall not be careful in the year of drought, neither shall cease from yielding fruit."

Day 15: Refilled by the Father

☐ Scripture:

Isaiah 40:29-31 (KJV)

He giveth power to the faint; and to them that have no might he increaseth strength. Even the youths shall faint and be weary, and the young men shall utterly fall: But they that wait upon the Lord shall renew their strength; they shall mount up with wings as eagles; they shall run, and not be weary; and they shall walk, and not faint.

Day 16 – Sow Anyway

☐ Scripture:

"They that sow in tears shall reap in joy."
— Psalm 126:5 (KJV)

Day 17 – The Harvest is His

☐ Scripture:

"So then neither is he that planteth any thing, neither he that watereth; but God that giveth the increase."
— 1 Corinthians 3:7 (KJV)

Day 18: It's Not Wasted

☐ Scripture:

"Therefore, my beloved brethren, be ye stedfast, unmoveable, always abounding in the work of the Lord, forasmuch as ye know that your labour is not in vain in the Lord."
-1 Corinthians 15:58 (KJV)

Day 19: Steady in the Stillness

☐ Scripture:

"The Lord shall fight for you, and ye shall hold your peace."
- Exodus 14:14 (KJV)

Day 20: *Tired but Trusting*

⬜ Scripture:

"God is our refuge and strength, a very present help in trouble."
- Psalm 46:1 (KJV)

Day 21: *Even When It's Not Fair*

⬜ Scripture:

"For I reckon that the sufferings of this present time are not worthy to be compared with the glory which shall be revealed in us."
-Romans 8:18 (KJV)

Day 1: *Peace in the Pressure*

Scripture:

"Be careful for nothing; but in every thing by prayer and supplication with thanksgiving let your requests be made known unto God.
And the peace of God, which passeth all understanding, shall keep your hearts and minds through Christ Jesus."
— Philippians 4:6–7 (KJV)

Reflection:

There are days when the weight of life feels unbearable — when responsibilities stack like bricks on your chest and the noise of the world drowns out the whisper of God. You wake up already behind. The bills are due, the children need you, the ministry pulls at your time, and your soul? Tired.

I remember a time early in ministry when we had to move—suddenly and unexpectedly. We were being called out of comfort and into the unknown, and I didn't want to go. We had to leave what felt safe and familiar with no clear destination, no plan, and very little money. I was pastoring a small church, earning $1300 a month, trying to care for my wife and four children.

In the chaos of packing and uncertainty, everything came crashing down. I stood in a house full of boxes and scattered belongings, the pressure building with every unpaid bill and unspoken fear. I walked outside, hid behind my truck, and screamed. I hit the side of it. I felt completely abandoned—by people, by peace… even, for a moment, by God. It wasn't the first time I'd broken under the pressure, and it wouldn't be the last. But in that moment, for the first time, I truly *relied* on the peace of God to carry me.

Peace didn't come because the situation changed right away. It came because God met me in the *middle* of the pressure. Peace came as I cried out and surrendered—not in strength, but in desperation. And true to His promise, He showed up. Quietly. Faithfully. Powerfully.

Paul reminds us: *Be careful for nothing.* That doesn't mean ignore your pain — it means don't carry it alone. God's peace doesn't make sense to the world. It's the kind of calm that can live inside chaos. That's the peace God offers — and it still holds today.

🙏 Prayer:

Lord, You see the pressure I'm under. You know the thoughts that overwhelm me and the things I try to carry in silence. Help me to release every burden into Your hands. Exchange my anxiety for Your peace. Calm my spirit, quiet my mind, and remind me that I am held. In Jesus' name, amen.

Journal Prompt:

What pressure are you carrying today that you haven't yet laid before God in prayer? Write it out — and then surrender it.

Day 2: *When It's All Too Much*

Scripture:

"Come unto me, all ye that labour and are heavy laden, and I will give you rest.
Take my yoke upon you, and learn of me; for I am meek and lowly in heart: and ye shall find rest unto your souls.
For my yoke is easy, and my burden is light."
— Matthew 11:28–30 (KJV)

Reflection:

There comes a point when you've given all you can — and it still isn't enough. The weight of expectations, responsibilities, and emotions press so hard that breathing feels like labor. The pressure becomes more than mental; it turns physical. Tight chest. Heavy limbs. Silent tears.

I remember when my wife's father was nearing the end of his life. We stayed in another town so she could be with him every moment. I was driving 45 minutes one way every day — balancing work, ministry, and caring for our four kids. I fixed supper, took on homeschooling (as best I could), and tried to keep everything together. It was exhausting. The kids weren't thrilled with dad stepping into mom's role, and the emotional toll of watching someone we loved suffer added a deep weight to every day life.

There were days I didn't want to get in the car. I didn't want to go to work. I didn't want to smile at church.

I was straining at every relationship I had. I was stretched so thin I thought I might snap.

But Jesus doesn't ask us to be strong on our own. He invites the weary. The ones who are worn out from doing good. The ones who feel like they're barely holding on.

"Come unto me…" That's not a cold command — it's a compassionate call. Jesus sees the burden you're under and offers you a divine trade: His strength for your struggle, His rest for your weariness.

Sometimes, rest doesn't look like a vacation or a day off. It looks like surrender. It looks like collapsing into the arms of a Savior who won't shame you for being tired. His yoke is easy — not because life is light, but because *He carries it with you.*

You don't have to hold it all together. Just come.

🙏 Prayer:

Jesus, I'm tired. My mind, my heart, my body — they're all worn thin. I don't want to pretend to be strong today. I want to rest in You. Remind me that You aren't disappointed in my weakness — You're inviting me to find strength in You. Teach me to release, surrender, and trust. Amen.

Journal Prompt:

What is one area of your life where you're running on empty? What would it look like to bring that exhaustion to Jesus today?

Day 3: *When You Feel Forgotten*

Scripture:

"Can a woman forget her sucking child, that she should not have compassion on the son of her womb? yea, they may forget, yet will I not forget thee.

Behold, I have graven thee upon the palms of my hands; thy walls are continually before me."

— Isaiah 49:15–16 (KJV)

Reflection:

There's a quiet kind of pain that creeps in when you feel unseen — when your faithfulness goes unnoticed, your effort goes unthanked, and your presence feels more like background noise than a blessing.

I remember one night as a teenager when I just needed someone to talk to. I didn't have a father in the home, and I was driving around in my truck just needing to vent — needing to *feel heard*. My youth director had always told me I was welcome to stop by anytime, no invitation needed. So I did.

But when I pulled up, I saw my best friend there. He was inside with a group of people jamming out — just being the guy everyone naturally gravitated to. He was incredibly gifted, good at everything he touched. And while I was grateful for his friendship, there were so many moments like this one where I felt like the moon to his sun — always around, but never the center.

That night, I drove away. What I needed was a conversation, but what I felt was forgotten. And that feeling — of showing up vulnerable, only to be invisible — left a mark.

Maybe you've been there. Maybe you're there now.

But Isaiah 49 reminds us that even if the most nurturing person in the world could forget you — *God never will.* You are engraved on His hands. Not penciled in. Not scribbled on a calendar. *Engraved.* Carved into the very place He holds you.

You are not forgotten. Not by the One who matters most.

Even when people overlook your effort or miss the ache behind your smile — God sees it all. And He remembers every single part of you.

🙏 Prayer:

God, when I feel invisible, remind me that I am engraved on Your hands. Thank You for seeing me when no one else does. For holding me close when I feel far away. For never forgetting me. Help me walk today with the quiet confidence that I am loved, known, and remembered. Amen.

Journal Prompt:

Have you felt forgotten in this season? What's one way you can remind your heart that God sees you, even if others don't?

Day 4: *Trusting in the Middle*

Scripture:

"Trust in the Lord with all thine heart; and lean not unto thine own understanding.

In all thy ways acknowledge him, and he shall direct thy paths."

— Proverbs 3:5–6 (KJV)

Reflection:

There's a unique pressure in not knowing. Not knowing how you'll pay that bill. Not knowing if the plan will work. Not knowing what's next, or when the next answer is coming. Sometimes, all you've got left is "Lord, help."

We like control. We like plans. But trust isn't forged in clarity — it's grown in the dark. It's born when there *isn't* a safety net. When everything in you says, "This makes no sense," and God says, "Trust Me anyway."

When we left the first church I pastored, it was a full-on leap of faith. I loved the congregation. I didn't want to leave. I had a wife and four kids depending on me — and we had *nowhere* to go. No home lined up. No income. Just an instruction from God: **Go.**

We moved in with my sister and her family, she was AWESOME — she made space for us even though her home wasn't really big enough. It was tight, uncomfortable, and uncertain. We were in the waiting — and it was hard. But then, a church nearly 3 hours away reached out, asking if I would consider being their pastor. It wasn't what I had imagined. I had hoped for a fresh start in another state — but this was only 45 minutes from my home church.

Still, everything about it had God's fingerprints on it. There was a parsonage — something we had never had before. And it had *everything* my wife had prayed for in a home. It was clear: God had written the story. We just had to trust Him with the pages we hadn't read yet.

Maybe you're in that kind of place right now — the middle, the in-between. If so, take heart: God's not just at the destination. He's in the waiting room with you, writing something beautiful.

🙏 Prayer:

Father, help me to trust You in the middle. When I can't see the way forward, remind me that You're already there, preparing a path. Teach me to lean on You — not my own plans, fears, or understanding. Give me peace in the uncertainty. Amen.

Journal Prompt:

Where in your life are you facing uncertainty? What would it look like to surrender control and trust God with that situation?

Day 5: *When You're Worn Out*

Scripture:

"And let us not be weary in well doing: for in due season we shall reap, if we faint not."
— Galatians 6:9 (KJV)

Reflection:

There's a kind of exhaustion that's hard to explain. It doesn't come from doing wrong — it comes from doing right. Showing up. Giving your all. Serving people who don't always serve back. Loving people who sometimes don't love you in return.

I remember my pastor told me before I ever stepped into ministry:

"If you can do anything else and be happy, do it."
He wasn't trying to discourage me — he was warning me. Pastoring isn't for the faint of heart. And it's not for part-timers. It's a calling that demands everything — your time, your energy, your heart, your home, your family.

Over the years, I've been on the receiving end of gossip, slander, and painful criticism. People have insulted my wife. Made passive-aggressive comments. Tried to undercut the vision God gave me because they didn't agree with how I led. I've had people withdraw from ministry just to make a statement — hoping it would push me out.

And yes, in those moments, I've thought about what my old pastor said. *"Could I do something else and be happy?"* I've asked God that question more than once. I've even thought about leaving ministry to find a "normal" job — one with fewer wounds, fewer expectations, less weight.

But then I remember…

It's not about being happy.

It's about being **faithful**.

It's about being obedient even when you don't want to be.

It's about trusting that God sees — even when no one else seems to.

If you're tired from the work of doing good, from staying faithful, from standing when it would be easier to sit down… don't give up. The promise still stands: *"In due season we shall reap, if we faint not."*

🙏 Prayer:

Lord, You see when I'm tired — not from doing wrong, but from trying to do right. You know the pressure of leading, loving, and living faithfully when it feels like no one understands. Give me renewed strength today. Help me to stay the course and not faint. Thank You for calling me — and for carrying me through the weariness. Amen.

Journal Prompt:

Write about a time when you were tempted to quit something good. What helped you keep going? What does "being faithful" look like for you right now?

_____

_____

_____

_____

_____

_____

_____

_____

_____

_____

Day 6: *When Doubt Creeps In*

Scripture:

"Now faith is the substance of things hoped for, the evidence of things not seen."
— Hebrews 11:1 (KJV)

📄 Reflection:

Pressure has a way of shaking what you *thought* you were sure of.

You believe you're called — until things go sideways.

You know God's promises — but the delay makes you second-guess.

You're confident in your role — until someone else questions it.

And then suddenly, the doubts creep in:

"Am I even doing this right?"

"Did God really call me?"

"What if I'm the wrong person for this?"

I've always had questions — about the Bible, about God, about Jesus, about Christianity, about everything. There was a time when no one wanted to answer them, and then a time when people tried but I didn't want to listen. I doubted Christianity for a long time — even while living a life that said otherwise.

At 16, I knew without a doubt that I was called into ministry. I preached for the first time at my home church, and even though I don't remember what I said, I remember the clarity: *This is what I'm supposed to do.* But like many do when they're young and scared of the weight of calling, I ran. I doubted. I wrestled.

I thought, *"Is this even real?"*

"How can I do this with the life I'm living?"

The pressures I was under made it feel impossible to believe that someone like me could ever stand in the ministry. Because deep down, I wasn't even sure I believed in the God of the Bible.

Fast forward. My mother-in-law — a woman of great faith — was sick and dying of cancer. I dreaded her passing, not just because of the pain it would bring our family, but because I had seen and heard some of the stories of the worst of people in moments like this — the fights, the tension, the drama that so often surrounds death. But I was wrong.

What I saw was a love lived out — a love that could only come from Jesus. It changed the way I saw life.

More importantly, it changed the way I saw *God.*

Because in that season, He changed *me.*

Almost a year later, I found myself sitting under a tent at a revival in my hometown. And God cornered me — lovingly, powerfully, unmistakably. He showed me that running wasn't an option anymore. And I answered the call to preach right then and there. I haven't looked back.

Faith isn't about never having questions. It's about trusting in the middle of them. It's not the absence of doubt — it's the decision to keep saying *yes* to God even when you can't see how it's all going to work out.

🙏 Prayer:

Father, thank You for being patient with my doubts. When I don't understand, help me to trust anyway. Remind me of my calling. Draw me back when I run. And help me to stand, not on what I see — but on who You are. Amen.

📝 Journal Prompt:

What doubts have been living under the surface of your faith? What truths has God shown you in the middle of your questions?

📖 Day 7: *Rest in His Peace*

Scripture:

"Peace I leave with you, my peace I give unto you: not as the world giveth, give I unto you. Let not your heart be troubled, neither let it be afraid."
— John 14:27 (KJV)

📝 Reflection:

There are moments in life when we are forced to let go. Not because we want to, but because we have no other choice.

In 2020, during the height of COVID-19, I found myself in that exact place. Like many, I didn't take it too seriously at first — until I got sick. Really sick. I thought I'd shake it off like a bad cold, but instead, I ended up in the hospital, barely able to breathe. My oxygen dropped so low, the doctors feared the worst. I was moved to ICU, hooked up to machines, stuck with needles, given transfusions — and isolated from everyone I loved.

No wife.
No kids.
No comfort — other than a video call and a song I played every day: *"Just Be Held"* by Casting Crowns.

I was helpless. I had zero control.
And that's when I discovered what it really meant to rest in

the peace Jesus gives.

It wasn't the kind that promised a fast fix. It was the kind that *held me* through the storm.

Jesus doesn't give peace like the world gives. The world's peace depends on circumstances. His peace shows up when you're surrounded by machines and uncertainty and fear — and *holds you anyway*.

Let go. Release the need to understand or fix everything. Rest in the hands of the One who's holding you even now.

🙏 Prayer:

Jesus, thank You for holding me when I couldn't hold myself. Thank You for peace that doesn't depend on my strength, but on Your presence. Help me to release what I can't control, and rest in the truth that You are enough. Amen.

Journal Prompt:

Where in your life do you feel the pressure to be in control? What would it look like to fully release that area to God and let Him hold you through it?

Day 8: *When You Feel Behind*

Scripture:

"The steps of a good man are ordered by the Lord: and he delighteth in his way."
— Psalm 37:23 (KJV)

Reflection:

About five months after I answered the call to ministry, a very good friend of mine answered his. It was never said out loud, but it *always felt* like we were in competition. He was ordained almost immediately. I had to wait over a year. He was brought into a big ministry quickly; I stayed at my home church, waiting for someone — anyone — to call and ask me to speak.

It was discouraging. Our families would comment on how quickly things were moving for him and ask, "Why aren't you already where he is?" I didn't have an answer. I was frustrated — even combative at times. I started comparing everything. I would record my sermons just to see how long they were compared to his or others, measuring my success by how long I preached. (Spoiler: not a great metric.)

It wasn't just him. *Every other minister* felt like they were lightyears ahead of me. I felt inferior and constantly driven to prove myself. It led to a lot of long, depressing nights.

But looking back now? I see what I couldn't then.

Psalm 37:23 says that "the steps of a good man are ordered by the Lord." Not the leaps. Not the accolades. The *steps*.

God wasn't holding me back — He was building me differently. Slower, maybe. Quieter, maybe. But intentionally. He was ordering every moment of my preparation, carving out character where I was trying to grasp at titles. I wasn't behind. I was being led.

And if you feel like everyone else is moving forward while you're standing still, remember this: the world rushes. God orders.

🙏 Prayer:

Father, thank You for ordering my steps, even when it feels like others are moving faster. Help me to release comparison and find confidence in Your timing. Teach me to trust the preparation and rest in the knowledge that I'm not behind — I'm in Your hands. In Jesus' name, Amen.

Journal Prompt:

Think of a time you compared your journey to someone else's. What emotions came up? What truths from God's Word can help you reframe that experience now?

_____

_____

_____

_____

_____

_____

_____

_____

_____

_____

Day 9: Success Redefined

Scripture:

"But he that is greatest among you shall be your servant."
— Matthew 23:11 (KJV)

Reflection:

It's easy to get it twisted — to mix up worldly success with Godly success. Deep down, I've always wanted my name to be known. When I first stepped into ministry, I dreamed of being the one every church wanted to book, the one with the answers, the voice of authority in every conversation. I wanted to be *the guy* — respected, requested, recognized.

I was chasing the wrong version of success.

The disciples did the same. Right after Jesus told them He was about to die, they broke into an argument about who would be the greatest among them. Can you imagine? The Savior is speaking of His sacrifice, and they're debating rank.

We are, by nature, selfish. We want to be seen.

But then I read a quote — shared by a pastor friend — that completely shifted my perspective. I don't remember who said it originally, but it went something like this:

"You worry about the depth and integrity of your ministry, and let God worry about the width and platform of it."

That line changed everything for me.

I realized I don't bring the increase. I don't control the growth. My job is not to expand my influence — it's to deepen my obedience.

God calls us to serve, not to strive. Whether I'm preaching on Sunday, helping someone at our nonprofit, or simply listening to a friend who feels forgotten — *that* is ministry. That is success in the Kingdom.

It's a humbling thing to lead through service. It doesn't always come with applause or visibility. But it pleases the heart of God.

So today, ask yourself: are you chasing attention or faithfulness? Are you trying to be great, or are you willing to serve?

🙏 Prayer:

Father, forgive me for the times I've chased visibility over obedience. Help me to define success the way You do — through humility, service, and surrender. Teach me to lead by example, to care more about the depth of my walk with You than the size of my platform. I trust You to bring the increase. In Jesus' name, amen.

In what areas of your life have you been striving for recognition? How can you shift your focus today from *being seen* to *being faithful*?

Day 10: Beauty in the Brokenness

Scripture:

"But he said to me, *My grace is sufficient for thee: for my strength is made perfect in weakness.* Most gladly therefore will I rather glory in my infirmities, that the power of Christ may rest upon me."

— 2 Corinthians 12:9 (KJV)

Reflection:

I mess things up. Over and over again. There are days I look at my life, my choices, even my ministry, and wonder, *How could God still use me?* I've carried shame, guilt, and the nagging feeling that I've just gone too far, failed too often, or disappointed Him too deeply.

And yet — He keeps picking me up.

The longer I serve, the more amazed I am at how far God is willing to go to redeem the broken things. When I was younger, a friend introduced me to a song by The Talley's called *"He Loves the Broken Ones."* That lyric has stayed with me because it's true. God isn't looking for the polished and perfect. He's looking for the surrendered.

I've seen it in my own life. Every time I've fallen short, every time I've wanted to give up, God has taken those shattered pieces and used them to build something stronger — not because of me, but in spite of me.

The truth is, when we finally admit just how broken we are, that's when God really starts to work. That's when pride falls away and grace moves in. That's when His strength is made perfect — not in our ability, but in our surrender.

He loves the broken ones. He uses the broken ones. He restores the broken ones.

You are not disqualified. You're exactly who He came for.

🙏 Prayer:

Father, thank You for loving me even in my most broken moments. I bring You all the pieces today — the ones I'm proud of and the ones I'm ashamed of. Use them for Your glory. Remind me that it's not about being perfect, it's about being available. Thank You for grace that runs deeper than failure. In Jesus' name, amen.

Journal Prompt:

Where in your life have you felt too broken to be used?
Write it out — and then ask God to show you how He can
use even *that* for His glory.

Day 11: *Called, but Not Always Comfortable*

Scripture:

"But the Lord said unto me, Say not, I am a child: for thou shalt go to all that I shall send thee, and whatsoever I command thee thou shalt speak.

Be not afraid of their faces: for I am with thee to deliver thee, saith the Lord."

— Jeremiah 1:7–8 (KJV)

Reflection:

I've been blessed to speak to many types of people— church members, deacons, pastors, community leaders. I've spoken in front of groups as small as fifteen and as large as a hundred or more. No matter the size or setting, the same feeling always hits me right before I step up: *What makes me qualified to speak to these people?*

That kind of pressure can be paralyzing. My oldest son has even said he doesn't understand how I—or any speaker—can get up in front of so many people and do what we do. And the truth is, I get nervous every single time. I have little nervous tics I do before every message. The nerves never really go away.

But what I've learned is this: it's not about me.

It's not about how qualified *I* feel. It's not about how confident *I* am. It's not even about how good *I* think the message is. It's about *God*. It's His word, His message, His power. I'm just the vessel.

When God called Jeremiah, He didn't say, "Convince them with your strength." He said, "Say not, I am a child... I am with thee." He reminded Jeremiah, as He reminds us, that calling doesn't require comfort—it requires obedience.

So when I step on that stage, or into that pulpit, I don't lean on my ability—I lean on His.

🙏 Prayer:

Lord, thank You for calling me despite my fears. Help me to remember it's not about my strength, but Yours. Give me peace in uncomfortable moments and boldness in the face of doubt. Speak through me and remind me that I am just the vessel—You are the message. Amen.

Journal Prompt:

When has fear or feeling unqualified held you back from walking in your calling? How would it change your perspective if you truly believed God goes before you and speaks through you?

📖 Day 12: *Faith in the Fog*

Scripture:

(For we walk by faith, not by sight:)
— 2 Corinthians 5:7 (KJV)

➤ Reflection:

In 2024, a massive hurricane swept through our area. We had just returned home from a trip—completely exhausted—when the storm hit harder than we expected. In the middle of the night, the power went out. It was pitch dark. I couldn't see my hand in front of my face. The wind howled so fiercely it sounded like the roof would tear off at any moment.

I woke up disoriented and panicked. *Where are my kids? My wife? Are we going to be okay?* I stumbled through the dark trying to find a light. We finally got to a flashlight and an old oil lamp. No one could sleep. The house creaked, the storm screamed—but eventually, morning came. Light came.

Sometimes following God feels like that—pitch-black, storm-howling, can't-see-the-next-step kind of living. It's easy to walk when the skies are clear. But when all you've got is the promise that He's still leading you? That's *faith in the fog*.

God never asked us to walk by what we can see. He asked us to walk by faith. Through storms. Through silence. Through fear. And the beauty is—He never leaves us to wander alone. Even in the darkness, He's guiding every step.

🙏 Prayer:

Lord, when I can't see where I'm going, help me trust where You're leading. Teach me to walk by faith and not by sight. Remind me that even when it's dark, You are still God—and You are still good. Amen.

Journal Prompt:

What "fog" are you currently walking through in your life? What would it look like to trust God with the next step, even if you can't see the full path?

Day 13: *When the Applause Fades*

Scripture:

"And whatsoever ye do, do it heartily, as to the Lord, and not unto men;"

— Colossians 3:23 (KJV)

📑 Reflection:

When you preach your heart out in front of a congregation, you're not looking for accolades—you're looking for results. You're hoping to see lives changed, hearts softened, souls stirred. You want to witness a spiritual move of God.

But more often than not, you're met with yawns, a few dozing heads, blank stares, folded arms, and sometimes even outright frustration on faces. You watch people rush to the door the moment the final "Amen" is said—not toward the altar, but toward the parking lot, hoping to beat the line at the local buffet.

As a pastor or speaker, it can be completely disheartening. You pour out everything inside of you, only to feel like it fell flat. But then I remember: I'm not preaching *to* them, I'm preaching *for* Him.

Jesus is the one who sends the Holy Spirit. Jesus is the one who brings the increase. Jesus is the one who works in the hearts and minds of the people sitting in those pews. My job is simply to be faithful.

Yes, it can feel soul-crushing when there are no visible results. When the altar stays empty. When no one stops to say "good word" or "that helped me." But true faithfulness isn't about recognition—it's about obedience. If I'm looking for applause, I've missed the point.

When I realign my heart to serve for *His* glory, not the approval of people, it changes my entire perspective. The applause might fade, but the call remains. And faithfulness is never wasted in the eyes of God.

🙏 Prayer:

Lord, help me to serve You with all my heart—even when no one's watching. Teach me not to crave the applause of people, but to be faithful for Your glory alone. Amen.

Journal Prompt:

When have you felt unnoticed or unappreciated in your calling? How can you remind yourself that your service is for God, not people?

Day 14: *Strong Enough to Stay*

Scripture:

Jeremiah 17:7-8 (KJV)

"Blessed is the man that trusteth in the Lord, and whose hope the Lord is. For he shall be as a tree planted by the waters, and that spreadeth out her roots by the river, and shall not see when heat cometh, but her leaf shall be green; and shall not be careful in the year of drought, neither shall cease from yielding fruit."

Reflection:

"Grow where you're planted." This is what my home pastor told me before I ever stepped into ministry. It's what he reminded me when I was deep in it—struggling with criticism, facing tough personalities, and navigating the undercurrent of church politics. Over and over again, that phrase was his answer when things felt like too much to bear.

And honestly, I've clung to it. When I wanted to pack it up and be done, when the ministry felt lonely or thankless, when the people I was pouring into were the same ones talking behind my back... I remembered his words: "Grow where you're planted. God will bring the increase."

Ministry isn't always a new place, a big title, or a large crowd. Sometimes the most powerful growth happens in the places that feel small and unseen. You don't have to move to matter. You just have to be faithful where He placed you. Because if God planted you there, He intends to do something with the soil beneath your feet.

🙏 Prayer:

Father, remind me that where You have me is not by accident. Give me the strength to stay rooted when it would be easier to run. Help me grow in this season, even if it feels dry or discouraging. I trust You to bring the increase—my job is to remain faithful. Amen.

Journal Prompt:

Where in your life do you feel tempted to give up or move on? How might God be asking you to "stay and grow" in that space? What does faithfulness look like for you right now?

Day 15: *Refilled by the Father*

Scripture:

Isaiah 40:29-31 (KJV)

He giveth power to the faint; and to them that have no might he increaseth strength. Even the youths shall faint and be weary, and the young men shall utterly fall: But they that wait upon the Lord shall renew their strength; they shall mount up with wings as eagles; they shall run, and not be weary; and they shall walk, and not faint.

➦ Reflection:

This verse was my father-in-law's favorite. I can still hear him talking about it, his voice steady and sincere as he recited it. It's a verse that has carried many through weariness—and it's carried me, too.

It is very easy to get discouraged, to get run down, to let life drain us in everything we do. We live in a world that constantly demands more from us—more time, more energy, more strength. And eventually, if we try to meet those demands on our own, we run dry. We weren't created to get our fulfillment from this world, but from Him, and in His way.

There are times in ministry, in parenting, in work, in life—where you feel completely empty. You wake up exhausted, and by noon you're already running on fumes.

You've poured out everything you have, and there's just... nothing left.

But if we are in Him, wait on Him, and do things according to His ways, we find strength we never knew was there. We are refilled, revitalized, renewed.

Being empty isn't the problem. Staying empty is. We aren't meant to be our own source of strength. He's the well that never runs dry. He gives strength to the faint. He renews those who wait on Him—not those who strive harder or fake being okay—but those who surrender and wait.

You don't have to be everything to everyone. You just have to sit at His feet and let Him pour back into what's been poured out. Because when you're refilled by the Father, you rise again—not on your own power, but on His.

🙏 Prayer:

Lord, I'm tired. I've tried to do it all, and I'm running on empty. Remind me that it's okay to stop and wait on You. Fill me again with Your strength, Your peace, and Your purpose. Help me to rest in You today. Amen.

Journal Prompt:

Where in your life are you feeling the most empty or drained? What would it look like to let God refill you in that area?

Day 16 – *Sow Anyway*
Scripture:
"They that sow in tears shall reap in joy."
— Psalm 126:5 (KJV)

Reflection:

I have planted many gardens in my day. I've watched my Grandpa, my Papa plant them too. Sometimes the soil isn't what it needs to be. Sometimes it takes real work to make the ground ready. You have to pull weeds, remove rocks, till the soil, make sure it's got the right nutrients. And even then—you still don't know exactly what kind of crop you'll get when it's all said and done.

But still, you plant the seed. You do the work. You prepare the ground. You guard it. You sweat. You cry. You pray. You labor in faith, believing that something good will come. And when that fruit finally appears—when you see the produce of what you've faithfully tended—it's so rewarding.

That's the picture this scripture gives us: sowing in tears. Sometimes we plant while broken. Sometimes we labor while uncertain. But we don't stop sowing. Ministry, family, friendships, callings—all of them require consistent tending, even when the harvest isn't visible yet.

Your job is to sow. God's job is the growth. Sow anyway.

🙏 Prayer:

Father, thank You for the reminder that sowing is my act of faith, even when I don't see fruit right away. Help me to be faithful in preparing the ground You've placed me in. Strengthen me when I'm weary, and remind me that You bring the harvest in due time. May my tears not be wasted, but water the very seeds You've called me to plant. Amen.

Journal Prompt:

Where in your life have you been sowing with tears? Write about what you've planted, even if you haven't seen fruit yet. How can you recommit to sowing in faith, trusting God for the harvest?

Day 17 – The Harvest is His

Scripture:

"So then neither is he that planteth any thing, neither he that watereth; but God that giveth the increase."

— 1 Corinthians 3:7 (KJV)

Reflection:

I've used this reference in several devotions now— "God brings the increase." It comes from this very verse. The apostle Paul was addressing a serious issue in the Corinthian church. The people were placing their value and worth on who baptized them or led them to Christ, using it almost like a spiritual status symbol. How crazy is that?

Paul quickly rebukes them and sets the record straight. We are only laborers. We don't have the power to save or convert a single soul. We are workers together for the fruit of the Gospel—for the ripe harvest God will bring.

It's not about our name, our reputation, or our accomplishments. It's about being faithful to plant the seed, to water where we can, and to trust that He will do the rest. He brings the increase. He ripens the fruit. It is by His will and His power that lives are changed.

Our part is obedience. His part is transformation. When we let go of the pressure to "perform" and simply do our role with faithfulness, we walk in true Kingdom purpose.

🙏 Prayer:

Father, thank You for reminding me that I am not the source of the harvest. I am just a laborer in Your field. Help me to stay faithful in the planting and watering, and let me trust You to bring the increase. Remove any pride or pressure that tries to creep in, and help me remember it's all for Your glory. Amen.

Journal Prompt:

Have you ever felt discouraged by the lack of visible "fruit" in your ministry or life? Write about the areas where you've been sowing seeds and ask God to help you trust Him with the increase.

Day 18: It's Not Wasted

Scripture: 1 Corinthians 15:58 (KJV)

"Therefore, my beloved brethren, be ye stedfast, unmoveable, always abounding in the work of the Lord, forasmuch as ye know that your labour is not in vain in the Lord."

Reflection

Preaching to statues is difficult. You give it your all and nothing seems to happen. You get yawns, eye rolls, blank stares — maybe even some snoring. It's disheartening. Do you give up? Do you call it a day and head home?

What about outside of church — at work, in your business, in your home? You're doing your best. You're grinding through timelines, expectations, quality control, managing co-workers, employers, employees, customer service, payroll, accounts payable, accounts receivable… and it all feels like it's falling apart. Like you're stuck in a narrowing tunnel with no room to breathe.

Where do you go when the path is too tight to turn around? You go forward. You press on. The Word says your labor — your ministry, your job, your parenting, your calling — is not in vain when it's in Him. What feels wasted in your eyes is seen and valued in His. Your faithfulness doesn't go unnoticed by God. He's working even when it feels like nothing's moving. So stay steady. Keep going. Go straight through.

🙏 Prayer

Lord, help me press on even when the fruit isn't visible and the journey feels tight. Remind me that nothing done for You is ever wasted. Strengthen me to keep going, keep speaking, and keep serving, even when I feel stuck. Thank You for seeing and honoring every effort. In Jesus' name, Amen.

💬 Journal Prompt

What situation in your life right now feels like a "narrow tunnel"? How can today's scripture help you stay steadfast and keep going, even when you feel like giving up?

Day 19: Steady in the Stillness

Scripture: Exodus 14:14 (KJV)

"The Lord shall fight for you, and ye shall hold your peace."

Reflection

We always feel like we need to be in charge. We need to be the ones leading the front lines — no matter who or what the opposition is. When we have a problem, we think we have to be the one to solve it. If there's an enemy coming (or any kind of issue that needs to be dealt with), we step up thinking *I'm going to handle this myself.*

Almost like we don't trust anyone else. Like no one else is good enough. Or maybe we think, *This is my problem. I shouldn't bother anyone else with it.*
But that's not how God works.

Israel stood between Pharaoh's army and the Red Sea. Nowhere to go. Outnumbered. Outmatched. And God said: "Be still. Watch. I will fight."

This isn't the last time God tells His people to step aside — to watch as *He* delivers the victory. All throughout Scripture, God lets His people stand on the sidelines while *He* shows up and fights for them.

He fights for *you.*

Sometimes the pressure isn't for us to carry. Sometimes, the battle isn't ours to fight. The Word doesn't say *you* will win this. It says *the Lord* will. So if He's fighting, our job is to hold our peace and remain steady — even in the silence.

***

🙏 Prayer

Father, help me let go of the need to be in control. I confess that I often try to handle everything on my own. But today, I choose to trust You. Help me to rest in Your power, not my own plans. You are my defender. I will wait on You. In Jesus' name, Amen.

***

Journal Prompt

Where in your life are you trying to fight a battle that belongs to God? What would it look like to step back and truly trust Him to take over?

Day 20: *Tired but Trusting*

Psalm 46:1 (KJV)

"God is our refuge and strength, a very present help in trouble."

Reflection

Weariness takes all kinds of forms. I understand tired. I understand exhaustion. There are different forms of "being tired"—physical exhaustion, mental fatigue, emotional burnout—all of which take significant tolls on our bodies and souls.

There have been weeks when a day off didn't come for 14 days, sometimes even 21. As a teenager and young adult, I could stay up for days, full of adrenaline and passion, chasing after a project or idea I was excited about. But as I've grown older, the weight of responsibility, the toll of ministry, and the demands of everyday life have made rest not just necessary—but sacred. And when it doesn't come, when we keep pushing without pause, our bodies, minds, and spirits begin to show the cracks.

I remember during a particularly spiritually and physically exhausting season, I worked 40+ hours at my part-time job—on top of all the ongoing ministry work. That week our church hosted a Boston Butt fundraiser, which meant staying up all night. And it just so happened to fall on Easter weekend, which is when we did the Boston

Butt Fundraiser. This is one of the most spiritually demanding and emotionally meaningful times of the year, that meant preparing messages, helping with home projects, managing church responsibilities, organizing the food bank, and being ready to preach by 7 AM Easter Sunday. After this week of physically, mentally, and spiritually demanding needs, let's just say… I didn't rest much Saturday night. And that Sunday morning, getting out of bed felt like dragging myself out of a pit. I wasn't enthusiastic. I wasn't energized. But I Had a peace- I knew God was there.

I've learned that when I'm at my end, God isn't. When I've got nothing left to give, **He becomes my everything.** He is not just a help—He is a *very present* help. In the moment. In the mess. In the middle of exhaustion, He is our strength and refuge.

We don't have to muster up the energy to keep going on our own. Sometimes we just need to *rest on Him*. Let Him fight for us. Let Him carry the burden. Let Him be our source when we're empty.

🙏 Prayer

Father, I am tired. Not just physically, but deep in my soul. Thank You for being my refuge and strength when I am empty. Help me to lean on You more and more. Teach me how to rest in You, to let You carry the weight I wasn't made to bear.

Journal Prompt Where are you running on empty right now? Write down the areas of your life where you feel most worn out, and ask the Lord to meet you there with His strength.

Day 21: *Even When It's Not Fair*

Romans 8:18 (KJV)

"For I reckon that the sufferings of this present time are not worthy to be compared with the glory which shall be revealed in us."

Reflection

Life isn't fair. You can give your all to serve God, pour yourself out for people, live a life of integrity—and still suffer. Meanwhile, others who cut corners, mock the faith, or live only for themselves seem to coast through untouched. It can make you question everything. Why try so hard? Why keep being faithful?

As I said, life isn't always fair. In fact, sometimes it feels like it rarely is. You serve God with all your heart— you give Him your time, your energy, your worship, your work—and yet, the wicked prosper. The people who have no regard for the Lord or His ways seem to succeed, while you're just trying to make it through the day without falling apart.

But the apostle Paul reminds us: this isn't the end of the story. The pain, frustration, and hurt of this present time—they're real, but they're also temporary. They're not even worthy to be compared to the glory that's coming. And that glory isn't just some vague idea—it's the fulfillment of salvation through Jesus Christ.

Psalm 73:26 tells us, *"My flesh and my heart faileth"*—yes, life will wear you down. But God? He is the strength of your heart. He is enough. He's not just a helper; He's your portion. Your reward. Your sustainer. Your reason for getting up one more time and trying again.

We may never understand why things happen the way they do, why injustice seems to run rampant, or why pain often finds the ones trying their hardest to follow Jesus—but we can know this: He is enough. He is the strength we lack. And He sees every sacrifice, every tear, every moment you've chosen faithfulness even when it was hard.

We want justice, we want equality, we want "our portion." But we do not truly understand what we are saying when we declare these things. Our portion is judgment. Our justice is not God's justice. In fact, we are in the very middle of God's mercy. Because for us to get justice, equality, and all these things we call "fair," it would mean death and certain wrath and destruction from God.

But instead—He gives us mercy. And He becomes our strength and our portion through His Son, Jesus. And in His Son, there is nothing here that can compare to that glory.

🙏 Prayer

Lord, I admit I don't always understand why life feels so unfair. But I thank You that I don't have to carry the weight of it all. You see me. You know my heart. You are my portion and my peace. Help me to trust You when things don't make sense, and give me strength to keep going when I'm weary. Let my hope rest not in fairness, but in Your faithfulness. In Jesus' name, amen.

Journal Prompt

Have you ever questioned God's fairness during a difficult time? How can trusting in His mercy and future glory help shift your focus from what feels unfair now?

Final Thoughts

✦ Final Prayer

Father,
Thank You for whoever is reading this right now. Bless them. Rest on them. Use them. Show them that it's okay to fall under the pressure—because it is You who holds us up. Thank You for walking with me through the weight of it all. Thank You for being present when I felt alone, for being steady when I was shaken, and for offering peace when everything else felt overwhelming.
Help me to trust You more deeply, obey You more quickly, and love You more completely—even when it feels like I'm absolutely alone in the chaos.
Teach me to rest in Your presence, to breathe deeply in Your peace, and to remember that **You are always there.**

In Jesus' name, Amen.

✦ A Note from My Heart to Yours

If you're walking through a heavy season right now, let me say this clearly: **you are not alone.** I've felt the pressure, the panic, the exhaustion—and the fear of not measuring up. I know what it feels like to be faithful and still feel like you're barely holding it together.

But here's what I've learned: *God doesn't require perfection—He honors obedience.*
He shows up right in the middle of the mess, the questions, the weight. He's not asking you to carry it all. He's asking you to **trust Him to carry it with you.**

So breathe. Cry if you need to. Keep showing up, not because you have all the answers—but because you're holding onto the One who does.

✦ Keep Going

Take what you've read here and **live it**. Start small:

- Pause when the pressure builds.

- Breathe in His peace.

- Pray over your people.

- Obey when it's hard.

- Journal when your heart's heavy.

And above all—**keep being faithful in the chaos of calling, kids, and everyday life**. You're not alone. He sees you. He's with you. And He will finish the good work He started in you.

Scripture Reflection Pages

(You Write what you Feel)

Scripture Index

Day Scripture Reference

Day Scripture Reference

19   Psalm 46:1

20   Matthew 11:28-30

21   Romans 8:18

About the Author

William E. Jackson is a husband, father, pastor, and writer with a heart for people navigating the chaos of calling, kids, and everyday life. With years of ministry experience and a life marked by real-world responsibility, he brings a message of hope, peace, and steadfast faith in the middle of pressure. His down-to-earth reflections connect Scripture to the struggles of daily life, offering encouragement and truth for those who feel stretched thin but want to stay faithful.

When he's not serving in the church or writing, you'll find him spending time with his family, chasing big dreams with his wife, and showing up faithfully wherever God leads.

Follow more of his work at:

www.facebook.com/aplaceforyoupodcast

Are you carrying more than your soul can hold?
Ministry, marriage, parenting, calling—it's a lot. Some days you feel stretched thin. Other days, like you're about to break. But in the middle of the chaos, God offers something the world can't: peace that holds firm under pressure.

In *Peace in the Pressure*, pastor and father William E. Jackson shares 21 raw and personal devotionals for those who are doing their best to be faithful in the middle of life's hardest moments. Whether you're leading others or just trying to keep your family afloat, this devotional will remind you:

- Obedience doesn't always feel easy—but it's always worth it

- God's peace isn't the absence of pressure—it's His presence in it

- You're not alone, even when the weight is heavy

- You can rest, even when nothing around you feels still

Each day includes heartfelt reflections, a prayer, and space to process what God is showing you. Let this devotional speak to your soul—and give you the strength to keep going.

Peace is possible. Even here. Even now.

Made in the USA
Columbia, SC
03 June 2025

58796052R00064